THE PATRIOT PAPERS

Bursting with Fun Facts about America's Early Rebels

JJ Prior and Emilia Whippie Prior

APPLESAUCE · PRESS ·

KENNEBUNKPORT, MAINE

13-Digit ISBN: 978-1604336054

10-Digit ISBN: 1604336056

This book may be ordered by mail from the
publisher. Please include $4.95 for postage
and handling. Please support your local
bookseller first!

Books published by Cider Mill Press Book
Publishers are available at special discounts
for bulk purchases in the United States by
corporations, institutions, and other organizations.
For more information, please contact the publisher.

Applesauce Press Book Publishers
"Where good books are ready for press"
12 Spring Street
PO Box 454
Kennebunkport, Maine 04046

Visit us on the Web! www.cidermillpress.com

Design by Jon Chaiet

Cover photo credit: Shutterstock/JohnKwan

Printed in China

1 2 3 4 5 6 7 8 9 0

First Edition

PHOTO CREDITS: page 5, Wikimedia; page 6,
Shutterstock/Victorian Traditions; page 8,
Shutterstock/Joseph Sohm; page 9, Shutterstock/
alexsvirid; page 9, Shutterstock/Everett Historical;
page 10, Shuttterstock/Susan Law Cain; page 11,
Shutterstock/Stocksnapper; page 13, Shutterstock/
Everett Historical; page 14, Shutterstock/Nataleana;
page 15, Shutterstock, patrimonio designs ltd; page 16,
Shutterstock/Everett Historical; page 19, Shutterstock/
patrimonio designs ltd; pages 20 and 21,
Shutterstock/Everett Historical; page 22,
Shutterstock/Mark Grenier; page 23, Library of
Congress, LC-USZ62-6078; page 24, Shutterstock/Mike
Flippo; page 25, Shutterstock, Victorian Traditions;
page 27, Shutterstock/Everett Historical; page 28,
Library of Congress, LC-USZ62-59464; page 29,
Shutterstock/Sean Donohue Photo; page 31,
Shutterstock/Everett Historical; page 32,
Shutterstock/I. Pilon; page 33, Shutterstock/Everett
Historical; page 34, Library of Congress; page 36,
Shutterstock/David Smart; page 44, Shutterstock/
www.BillionPhotos.com; page 49, Shutterstock/Mark
Grenier; page 55, Shutterstock/Kovalchuk Oleksandr;
page 56, Shutterstock/Brandon Bourdages; page 59,
Shutterstock/I. Pilon; page 61, Shutterstock/Everett
Historical; page 63, Shutterstock/sergign; page 64,
Shutterstock/Everett Historical; page 65, Library of
Congress, LC-USZ62-68483; page 67, Shutterstock/
I. Pilon; page 71, Shutterstock/Susan Law Cain; page
72, Shutterstock/Everett Historical; page 74,
Shutterstock/Alexander Donchev; page 77,
Shutterstock/Balefire; page 81, Shutterstock/
Everett Historical; page 82, Library of Congress,
LC-DIG-pga-05287; page 84, Library of Congress,
LC-USZ62-25768; page 84, Library of Congress,
LC-USZ62-25768; page 85, Shutterstock/Everett
Historical; page 87, Library of Congress,
LC-DIG-ppmsca-15704; pages 88 and 89, Shutterstock/
Everett Historical; page 90, Library of Congress,
LC-USZ62-72497; page 92, Library of Congress,
LC-USZC2-3273; pages 94 and 96, Shutterstock/
Everett Historical; page 98, Library of Congress,
LC-USZC4-2542; pages 100, 102, and 104, Shutterstock/
Everett Historical; page 105, Library of Congress,
LC-USZC4-2791; and 106, Library of Congress,
LC-USZ62-68483.

CONTENTS

★★★★★★★★★★★★★★★★★★★★★★★★★★★★★★★★★★★★★

INTRODUCTION - 4

BACKGROUND ON THE DECLARATION
OF INDEPENDENCE - 6

*THE DECLARATION
OF INDEPENDENCE* - 10

UNDERSTANDING
THE CONSTITUTION - 28

*THE CONSTITUTION OF
THE UNITED STATES OF AMERICA* - 37

INTRODUCTION TO
THE BILL OF RIGHTS - 72

THE U.S. BILL OF RIGHTS - 75

THE PATRIOTS: BIOS OF
REVOLUTIONARY REBELS - 82

TEACHING WITH THIS BOOK - 108

ABOUT THE AUTHORS - 111

★★★★★★★★★★★★★★★★★★★★★★★★★★★★★★★★★★★★★

INTRODUCTION

What would you do if you felt you were being treated unfairly? Would you speak up? Who would you tell? And what would you do to make sure the problem gets fixed?

More than two centuries ago, in the year 1776, tensions were high in the British American colonies. Many colonists felt laws and actions placed on them by Britain's Parliament and King George III were unfair. These laws treated the people living in the colonies differently, even though they were all supposedly Englishmen. The colonists complained and protested, but nothing was done. It was time for drastic measures! They needed to be free from the rule of a king to allow all people to be treated in a fair way.

A group representing the colonies wrote an announcement that our new country would be free from the king and his country. Then, they created a plan to make sure the new country would stay free from unfair rule from within. Finally, these founders listed the ways that individual people in the United States would be protected from intrusive government control in their lives. These rights would apply to all people equally— a very fair system indeed!

Inside this book, we invite you to

FUN FACT

The colonies didn't decide to split from England out of the blue. The trouble began after King George III became king in 1760. By May 1776, eight colonies' legislatures had already voted to support independence.

explore three important documents that made our country what it is today: the Declaration of Independence, the U.S. Constitution, and the Bill of Rights. It is our hope that by reading and better understanding these documents you will know your rights as American citizens and know why these rights are important to keeping our society fair for all people.

BACKGROUND ON THE DECLARATION OF INDEPENDENCE

The Declaration of Independence was a big deal. For more than 150 years, people from Great Britain had been settling in the lands along the east coast of North America, an area nicknamed early on as the "New World." Early settlements in Jamestown and Plymouth grew and expanded to become whole colonies. As ships brought more people and as families grew and spread out, populations of dozens grew to hundreds of thousands over a century and a half. All throughout this time, thousands of miles across an ocean from their homeland, early American colonists considered themselves British people. They were largely loyal to the king, despite many having never even been to England.

As time went on, things got a little more complicated. England controlled trade with the colonies, so only British goods were allowed to be brought in to port. Keeping an army ready to fight in defense was expensive, so the English lawmakers known as Parliament made a law that colonists had to find or pay for places for soldiers to live. King George III and Parliament also thought they had the right to tax the colonies to pay off the debts, or money that was owed, as a result of a previous war. People had to pay taxes on hundreds of different items they wanted to buy.

The American colonists saw these difficulties add up over time. Some wanted to buy less expensive goods from places England didn't control. Some colonists thought the army was unnecessary since the war was over. And many didn't think it was fair to pay a tax that Parliament decided upon, when the colonies didn't have anyone to represent them and vote in Parliament.

People in the colonies started to push back by boycotting British goods—they just wouldn't buy them! At one point, a rowdy Boston crowd protested by dumping British tea into the harbor, right off the sides of the ships it came on.

Throughout it all, however, most people still saw themselves as subjects of the king. A large majority were undecided at best about cutting ties with England, and many held out hope for fixing the messy relationship.

The turning point came in January 1776 when a man named Thomas Paine wrote and published a 48-page pamphlet called *Common Sense,* arguing that independence was the only way to go. With nearly a half-million copies printed that year, *Common Sense* became the most widely read document of its day.

THIS TIMELINE SHOWS THE ORDER OF KEY EVENTS, BUT IT IS NOT TO SCALE.

MAY 1607 ★ Jamestown is established as the first permanent English settlement in the New World.

1600

General George Washington even had it read to his troops for inspiration.

Paine wrote *Common Sense* for the common people, in simple language that likely contributed to its success. Critical of monarchies, and particularly George III, *Common Sense* built up great support for an official separation from the motherland. Later that year, a group of delegates from each colony voted to move forward with just that: They would announce to the world that the American colonies no longer belonged to England.

PLAIN TRUTH;

ADDRESSED TO THE

INHABITANTS

OF

AMERICA,

Containing, Remarks

ON A LATE PAMPHLET,

entitled

COMMON SENSE:

Wherein are shewn, that the Scheme of INDEPENDENCE is Ruinous, Delusive, and Impracticable : That were the Author's Asseverations, Respecting the Power of AMERICA, as Real as Nugatory ; Reconciliation on liberal Principles with GREAT BRITAIN, would be exalted Policy : And that circumstanced as we are, Permanent Liberty, and True Happiness, can only be obtained, by HONORABLE CONNECTIONS, with that Kingdom.

WRITTEN BY CANDIDUS

Will ye turn from flattery, and attend to this Side. ?

There TRUTH, unlicenc'd, walks ; and dares accost Even Kings themselves, the Monarchs of the Free ! THOMSON on the Liberties of BRITAIN.

PHILADELPHIA:
Printed, and Sold, by R. BELL, in Third-Street.

MDCCLXXVI.

1620 ★ Plymouth is settled by the Pilgrims.

IN CONGRESS, JULY 4, 1776.

The unanimous Declaration of the thirteen united States of America.

1756 ★ French and Indian War pitted the colonies of British America in battle against New France for control of territory.

1750

The colonists' militias and army had been fighting British troops for over a year, and it was time to be official.

A five-man committee was tasked with drafting a letter saying that American colonists were going to separate from Britain and listed reasons why they felt breaking ties was necessary. Thomas Jefferson, a young lawyer from Virginia, was chosen to write the announcement. Jefferson wasn't writing about anything new. He was listing many of the frustrations that a majority of colonists had been feeling during the Revolutionary period. He later said, "I did not consider it as any part of my charge to invent new ideas." The purpose of the Declaration was "to place before mankind the common sense of the subject."

This document became known as the Declaration of Independence, and Americans recognize the date written at the top as our nation's birthday: July 4, 1776. Despite the long history and connection with England, from that point on America would stand on its own.

FUN FACT
The Declaration parchment measures 24½ inches across by 29¾ inches tall.

OCTOBER 25, 1760 ★ King George III ascends to the throne of England.

THE DECLARATION OF INDEPENDENCE

IN CONGRESS, July 4, 1776.

The unanimous Declaration of the thirteen united States of America,

When in the Course of human events, it becomes necessary for one people to dissolve the political bands which have connected them with another, and to assume among the powers of the earth, the separate and equal station to which the Laws of Nature and of Nature's God entitle them, a decent respect to the

1764 ★ Sugar Act tightened British control of the trade of goods in the colonies.

1765 ★ Facing a large bill for the French and Indian War, England begins taxing any printed paper such as official documents and newspapers. This Stamp Act even included a tax specifically for playing cards!

1764

opinions of mankind requires that they should declare the causes which impel them to the separation.

We hold these truths to be self-evident, that all men are created equal, that they are endowed by their Creator with certain unalienable Rights, that among these are Life, Liberty and the pursuit of Happiness.

-- That to secure these rights, Governments are instituted among Men, deriving their just powers from the consent of the governed,

-- That whenever any Form of Government becomes destructive of these ends, it is the Right of the People to alter or to abolish it, and to institute new Government, laying its foundation on such principles and organizing its powers in such form, as to them shall seem most likely to effect their Safety and Happiness.

We think it's obvious that people have certain rights and deserve to be free.

To make sure people's rights are protected, people can make a government.

If a government does bad things, we think people should change it or make a new one that is better.

MARCH 5, 1770 ★ A rowdy Boston crowd threw rocks and ice at British soldiers, and the soldiers fired their guns in defense, killing five Bostonians. The colonists quickly acted to make the soldiers look bad, claiming they killed peaceful people for no reason. The colonists even called it a "massacre" to make the event seem worse than it was.

It's a big deal to change your government, and you can't do it all willy-nilly. Most of the time people will just deal with it and let things that bug them keep happening. If you do change the government, you'd better have a really good reason!

Prudence, indeed, will dictate that Governments long established should not be changed for light and transient causes; and accordingly all experience hath shewn, that mankind are more disposed to suffer, while evils are sufferable, than to right themselves by abolishing the forms to which they are accustomed.

FUN FACT

To print copies of the signatures on the Declaration, a printer named William Stone may have pulled some ink from the original to make his printing press plate. It took Stone nearly three years to carefully carve all the words and signatures for printing!

FUN FACT

In its lifetime, the Declaration has been transported on horseback, by wagons, ships, a Pullman sleeper train car, and an armored vehicle.

MAY 10, 1773 ★ The Tea Act gave England a monopoly on taxed tea imports to the American colonies, further raising tensions.

But when a long train of abuses and usurpations, pursuing invariably the same Object evinces a design to reduce them under absolute Despotism, it is their right, it is their duty, to throw off such Government, and to provide new Guards for their future security.

-- Such has been the patient sufferance of these Colonies; and such is now the necessity which constrains them to alter their former Systems of Government. The history of the present King of Great Britain is a history of repeated injuries and usurpations, all having in direct object the establishment of an absolute Tyranny over these States.

usurp. v. to take illegally or by force

If the government keeps doing bad stuff over and over, it's important for people to stand up and make a change!

This is what's going on with us! The king has been doing unfair things to us for way too long and won't let anyone have control but himself!

DECEMBER 16, 1773 ★ To protest the British monopoly on imported tea, colonists took over ships moored in Boston harbor and tossed their contents—90,000 pounds of tea—overboard.

We've got proof! Listen up, everyone in the world. Here's a list of all the unfair stuff he's done.

assent. v. to approve or agree

The king won't approve the laws we come up with. (You know, the laws that protect rights!) He refused to pass a law abolishing the slave trade.

The king won't even let us have the most important laws until he agrees. (Sometimes he took years!)

To prove this, let Facts be submitted to a candid world.

★ He has refused his Assent to Laws, the most wholesome and necessary for the public good.

★ He has forbidden his Governors to pass Laws of immediate and pressing importance, unless suspended in their operation till his Assent should be obtained; and when so suspended, he has utterly neglected to attend to them.

FUN FACT

Only John Hancock, president of the congress, and Charles Thomson, secretary of the congress, signed on July 4. The copy they signed was the final wording that would be printed and distributed.

1774 ★ In response to the Boston Tea Party, the English Parliament ordered the port of Boston to be closed and took over complete control of the Massachusetts government. Other colonies feared these Intolerable Acts could happen to them as well.

1774

★ He has refused to pass other Laws for the accommodation of large districts of people, unless those people would relinquish the right of Representation in the Legislature, a right inestimable to them and formidable to tyrants only.

★ He has called together legislative bodies at places unusual, uncomfortable, and distant from the depository of their public Records, for the sole purpose of fatiguing them into compliance with his measures.

★ He has dissolved Representative Houses repeatedly, for opposing with manly firmness his invasions on the rights of the people.

★ He has refused for a long time, after such dissolutions, to cause others to be elected; whereby the Legislative powers, incapable of Annihilation, have returned to the People at large for their exercise; the State remaining in the mean time exposed to all the dangers of invasion from without, and convulsions within.

KING: "You can have that law, but you have to give up your right to vote."

COLONIST: "You're being a bully!"

FUN FACT
For many years, most of the general public didn't know Thomas Jefferson wrote the Declaration. Official records of Congress only indicated he was one of the committee of five who drafted it.

How can the courts be fair if the king writes the judges' paychecks?

We think the King made up new jobs for his soldiers, just to annoy us!

★ He has endeavoured to prevent the population of these States; for that purpose obstructing the Laws for Naturalization of Foreigners; refusing to pass others to encourage their migrations hither, and raising the conditions of new Appropriations of Lands.

★ He has obstructed the Administration of Justice, by refusing his Assent to Laws for establishing Judiciary powers.

★ He has made Judges dependent on his Will alone, for the tenure of their offices, and the amount and payment of their salaries.

★ He has erected a multitude of New Offices, and sent hither swarms of Officers to harrass our people, and eat out their substance.

SEPTEMBER–OCTOBER 1774 ★ Following the Intolerable Acts, delegates from most colonies met to decide how to respond. This First Continental Congress resulted in a boycott of British goods.

1774

★ He has kept among us, in times of peace, Standing Armies without the Consent of our legislatures.

★ He has affected to render the Military independent of and superior to the Civil power.

★ He has combined with others to subject us to a jurisdiction foreign to our constitution, and unacknowledged by our laws; giving his Assent to their Acts of pretended Legislation:

jurisdiction. n. the official power to make legal decisions in a place

★ For Quartering large bodies of armed troops among us:

★ For protecting them, by a mock Trial, from punishment for any Murders which they should commit on the Inhabitants of these States:

quartering. v. to provide a place of lodging for troops. In the case of the colonists, people were forced to open their homes to British soldiers

★ For cutting off our Trade with all parts of the world:

inhabitants. n. the people who live in a place

APRIL 18–19, 1775 ★ Paul Revere, Samuel Dawes, and William Prescott ride from Boston to warn the countryside of the advancing British army.

★ For imposing Taxes on us without our Consent:

★ For depriving us in many cases, of the benefits of Trial by Jury:

★ For transporting us beyond Seas to be tried for pretended offences

province. n. a political subdivision of a country. (Most countries call their smaller parts "provinces" the way the U.S. calls them "states.")

★ For abolishing the free System of English Laws in a neighbouring Province, establishing therein an Arbitrary government, and enlarging its Boundaries so as to render it at once an example and fit instrument for introducing the same absolute rule into these Colonies:

FUN FACT

John Adams convinced Thomas Jefferson that he should be the one to write the Declaration of Independence. He gave three reasons: "Reason first, you are a Virginian, and a Virginian ought to appear at the head of this business. Reason second, I am obnoxious, suspected, and unpopular. You are very much otherwise. Reason third, you can write ten times better than I can."

MAY 5, 1775 ★ The Second Continental Congress begins. It would create the Continental Army under the command of George Washington and take the steps toward Independence.

1775

- For taking away our Charters, abolishing our most valuable Laws, and altering fundamentally the Forms of our Governments:

- For suspending our own Legislatures, and declaring themselves invested with power to legislate for us in all cases whatsoever.

- He has abdicated Government here, by declaring us out of his Protection and waging War against us.

- He has plundered our seas, ravaged our Coasts, burnt our towns, and destroyed the lives of our people.

"George tried to get rid of all the great work we had done so far! What the heck!"

abdicate. v. the act of a monarch giving up power

"So, that means we've got to take matters into our own hands."

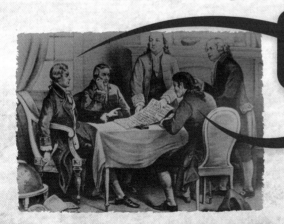

That might have been a little harsh, don't you think? King George didn't personally do all that.

Yeah, but this will really get people fired up!

FUN FACT
John Hancock signed the Declaration first because he was the president of the Second Continental Congress.

"King George is turning people against each other!"

★ He is at this time transporting large Armies of foreign Mercenaries to compleat the works of death, desolation and tyranny, already begun with circumstances of Cruelty & perfidy scarcely paralleled in the most barbarous ages, and totally unworthy the Head of a civilized nation.

★ He has constrained our fellow Citizens taken Captive on the high Seas to bear Arms against their Country, to become the executioners of their friends and Brethren, or to fall themselves by their Hands.

FUN FACT

Right after being approved by Congress, the Declaration headed over to John Dunlap's print shop in Philadelphia. Nobody knows how many copies he made, but 26 originals still exist today.

JUNE 17, 1775 ★ Though severely outnumbered, patriot fighters held off British forces for more than two hours in the first major battle of the revolutionary war, the Battle of Bunker Hill. The Bostonians had to give up and retreat, but they showed they could stand up to the experienced British army.

1775

- ★ He has excited domestic insurrections amongst us, and has endeavoured to bring on the inhabitants of our frontiers, the merciless Indian Savages, whose known rule of warfare, is an undistinguished destruction of all ages, sexes and conditions.

- ★ In every stage of these Oppressions We have Petitioned for Redress in the most humble terms: Our repeated Petitions have been answered only by repeated injury.

- ★ A Prince whose character is thus marked by every act which may define a Tyrant, is unfit to be the ruler of a free people.

insurrection. n. a violent attack or uprising against a government or authority

"The King is getting everybody else here riled up and causing even more trouble than he can create all by himself!"

"We've asked nicely, but clearly Georgie isn't a good listener."

redress. n. a remedy or compensation for harm done against someone

FUN FACT

The Declaration wasn't signed on July 4. Most delegates to Congress signed the engrossed parchment copy of the Declaration on August 2, 1776—a full month after voting to write it!

JULY 2, 1776 ★ The Continental Congress voted to support declaring independence from Great Britain. Then, Thomas Jefferson went to work on the final draft of the Declaration.

Nor have We been wanting in attentions to our British brethren. We have warned them from time to time of attempts by their legislature to extend an unwarrantable jurisdiction over us.

FUN FACT

When the British invaded Washington, D.C. in 1814, they set fire to important buildings—even the White House. Thankfully, the Declaration and other important documents had been gathered up and quickly taken out of town to safety—to be hidden in an old mill!

Most delegates of the Continental Congress thought we would celebrate July 2 as the date we declared independence. John Adams wrote to his wife Abigail: "The second day of July, 1776, will be the most memorable epoch in the history of America. I am apt to believe that it will be celebrated by succeeding generations as the great anniversary festival." So, why do we celebrate July 4? That's the date Congress approved the final language of the Declaration, and it's the date written on the top of the signed document.

JULY 4, 1776 ★ Congress votes to approve the final language of the Declaration.

JULY 12, 1776 ★ Second Continental Congress begins work on a new government in the Articles of Confederation.

We have reminded them of the circumstances of our emigration and settlement here. We have appealed to their native justice and magnanimity, and we have conjured them by the ties of our common kindred to disavow these usurpations, which, would inevitably interrupt our connections and correspondence. They too have been deaf to the voice of justice and of consanguinity.

consanguinity. n. a relationship sharing a common ancestor

DECEMBER 25, 1776 ★ General George Washington led his Continental Army troops across the Delaware River into New Jersey, where the army was able to gain two swift battle victories with the element of surprise in their favor.

> **"We gotta do what we gotta do!"**

acquiesce. v. to accept reluctantly

supreme. adj. superior to all others. In this case, the "Supreme Judge of the world" means God.

rectitude. n. morally correct behavior or thinking; righteousness

We must, therefore, acquiesce in the necessity, which denounces our Separation, and hold them, as we hold the rest of mankind, Enemies in War, in Peace Friends.

We, therefore, the Representatives of the united States of America, in General Congress, Assembled, appealing to the Supreme Judge of the world for the rectitude of our intentions, do, in the Name, and by Authority of the good People of these Colonies, solemnly publish and declare, That these United Colonies are, and of Right ought to be Free and Independent States;

FUN FACT
All colonies but New York voted to move forward with declaring independence on July 2. New York's delegates abstained, or didn't vote yes or no, because their home legislature hadn't given them directions to support independence.

SEPTEMBER–OCTOBER 1777 ★ British forces, led by General John Burgoyne, found themselves surrounded in upstate New York in what we know as the Battles of Saratoga. After two battles eighteen days apart and a week of negotiation, Burgoyne surrendered to the Americans.

1777

that they are Absolved from all Allegiance to the British Crown, and that all political connection between them and the State of Great Britain, is and ought to be totally dissolved; and that as Free and Independent States, they have full Power to levy War, conclude Peace, contract Alliances, establish Commerce, and to do all other Acts and Things which Independent States may of right do. And for the support of this Declaration, with a firm reliance on the protection of divine Providence, we mutually pledge to each other our Lives, our Fortunes and our sacred Honor.

absolve. v. to set free

allegiance. n. loyalty to a larger power

"It's over! We're moving on!"

Providence. n. the protective care of God

"Quit holding us back! We have a lot to do!"

FUN FACT
Thomas Jefferson wrote the wording of the Declaration, but the final document was likely engrossed, or handwritten, by Congress' clerk, Timothy Matlack.

DECEMBER 1777 ★ The Continental Army endured a long winter camped at Valley Forge under Washington's command. During this time, soldier training improved significantly and the army emerged stronger and better prepared to fight.

ARTICLES

OF

CONFEDERATION

AND

PERPETUAL UNION

BETWEEN THE

STATES

OF

NEW-HAMPSHIRE, MASSACHUSETTS-BAY, RHODE-ISLAND AND PROVIDENCE PLANTATIONS, CONNECTICUT, NEW-YORK, NEW-JERSEY, PENNSYLVANIA, DELAWARE, MARY-LAND, VIRGINIA, NORTH-CAROLINA, SOUTH-CAROLINA AND GEORGIA.

LANCASTER, (PENNSYLVANIA,) PRINTED:

BOSTON, RE-PRINTED BY JOHN GILL, PRINTER TO THE GENERAL ASSEMBLY, M,DCC,LXXVII.

Before the Constitution, the United States were loosely governed by this document, the Articles of Confederation.

1778

UNDERSTANDING THE CONSTITUTION

"It is much easier to pull down a Government, in Such a Conjunture of affairs as We have seen, than to build up, at such a Season as the present."
—John Adams in a letter to James Warren in 1787

The Constitution is more than a set of laws for our country. It's like an instruction manual for the whole government. After the colonies declared independence from England, the new states had to figure out who would be in charge and what those people would (and wouldn't) be allowed to do. This isn't an easy task! Since the colonies began, there had always been a king who was the ultimate authority. In our country today we know it works, but back when the new United States was just getting started, it was all just a big experiment.

FEBRUARY 1778 ★ After learning of the United States' victory in battle at Saratoga, France enters the war on the patriots' side.

Have you ever bought something that just didn't work right for you? Maybe it was a jacket that was too big, or the brakes on a bike didn't work. Sometimes things don't work out on the first try. Believe it or not, that's just what happened for the United States government!

Soon after declaring independence from Great Britain, members of the Second Continental Congress got together to start deciding how the country would run on its own. They wrote the Articles of Confederation, a plan that said all 13 states would keep running by themselves. (It even said Canada could join the country, if they wanted to.) Instead of a king or any one ruler, there would be a congress to make laws for the whole country. The problem was, Congress by itself didn't have much power. Congress had no power to raise money through taxes, and there was no executive or court to even enforce the laws that were made.

MARCH 1, 1781 ★ Maryland is the last state to ratify the Articles of Confederation.

For this reason, many people believed the Articles of Confederation were not an effective model for the United States to follow. It was a good first try for the young country that had never been without a monarch in charge, but it just wasn't working. After unrest in the states suggested a new plan was needed, in May 1787 some prominent Americans got back together for a convention. Their decision?

GO BACK TO THE DRAWING BOARD!

While waiting for everyone to get together, a delegate from Virginia named James Madison drafted a proposal that was different from the Articles of Confederation in many ways. The Virginia Plan designed the central government to be more powerful than the states. It took a lot of debate and revisioning, but by September 17, 1787 a new plan was ready. The United States had its new instruction manual.

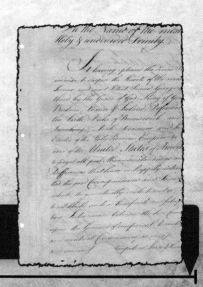

SEPTEMBER 3, 1783 ★ The Treaty of Paris formally ends the war.

FUN FACT

Not everyone liked the new Constitution. People in support of the Constitution were known as "Federalists," while those opposed were anti-Federalists. When Pennsylvania's assembly was set to vote on the Constitution, a couple anti-Federalist representatives stayed home so there wouldn't be a quorum, or enough people for an official vote. A rowdy mob of people stormed into their houses and dragged them to the state house so the vote could happen!

FUN FACT

Rhode Island's leaders refused to participate in the convention to write the Constitution. They were afraid it was a plan to overthrow the government and might hurt their way of life.

FUN FACT

Signers of the Declaration arranged their signatures based on the geographic location of their states. Being from the northernmost colony, New Hampshire delegates signed first after Hancock. Southernmost Georgia delegates ended the list.

SEPTEMBER 17, 1787 ★ Constitutional convention approves the language of the U.S. Constitution and sends it to the states for approval.

So what's in this instruction manual? First, there are the assembly directions. Since the government would truly be new in many ways, the writers of the Constitution carefully explained each of the parts and how they would work with each other. There are three big pieces that have to be put together, and each piece does a different job.

FUN FACT

James Madison, a congressional delegate from Virginia, became the careful note-taker of the 1787 convention. He wrote most of the Constitution himself. He later joked that spending so much time alone writing almost killed him!

JUNE 21, 1788 ★ After being ratified by nine states, the U.S. Constitution is established as the new governing document for the United States.

First, Congress would exist to make laws for the whole country. It would be made up of two groups of people who would be elected to represent each state, so people from every state would get a say in how the country is run. This is known as the **Legislative Branch.**

Once the laws are made, another branch of the government would execute the laws, or put them into action. The Constitution said a president would be in charge of this. What it didn't say was how the president would do it all—and there is a lot to do! Most of the things that have to be done by the government fall on the **Executive Branch.**

Finally, the Constitution's writers thought the only way to keep the laws fair for people was to have the court system be completely separate from other parts of government. The courts would make up the third branch of the government, known as the **Judicial Branch.**

SEPTEMBER 25, 1789
★ The first Congress of the United States proposed 12 amendments to the Constitution, outlining the rights of citizens that hadn't been stated in the original document.

There are other directions in this manual, such as what to do if a part breaks (if a president, judge, or member of Congress breaks the law) and even how to "update" the manual if changes (called amendments) need to be made. The Constitution is the "supreme Law of the Land," meaning no other instruction manual is more important!

Back in 1787 the United States was a bit of a new invention, still being tested. No one knew for sure if it would work or not! Today that machine is still running strong, and the people at the controls are still using the same instruction manual as their guide, the United States Constitution.

DECEMBER 15, 1791 ★ The first 10 amendments, known as the Bill of Rights, are adopted by Virginia, meaning three-fourths of the states required to amend the Constitution had ratified the changes.

THE CONSTITUTION OF THE UNITED STATES OF AMERICA

We the People of the United States, in Order to form a more perfect Union, establish Justice, insure domestic Tranquility, provide for the common defence, promote the general Welfare and secure the Blessings of Liberty to ourselves and our Posterity, do ordain and establish this Constitution for the United States of America.

union. n. two or more things that are joined together; in this case, states

tranquility. n. calm; peace

welfare. n. the health, happiness, and fortunes of a person or a group

posterity. n. the future generations of people; descendants

The famous first sentence of the Constitution is called the preamble. It lists the reasons the United States needs a government and set of laws, and why "the people" decided to make it.

ARTICLE 1.

SECTION 1

All legislative Powers herein granted shall be vested in a Congress of the United States, which shall consist of a Senate and House of Representatives.

> Article 1 tells us where our laws will come from: a Congress, made up of elected people.

> legislative. adj. having the power to make laws

SECTION 2

The House of Representatives shall be composed of Members chosen every second Year by the People of the several States, and the Electors in each State shall have the Qualifications requisite for Electors of the most numerous Branch of the State Legislature.

> Representatives need to be "seasoned" and local.

No Person shall be a Representative who shall not have attained to the Age of twenty five Years, and been seven Years a Citizen of the United States, and who shall not, when elected, be an Inhabitant of that State in which he shall be chosen.

FUN FACT

When the first election for president happened in 1788 and 1789, not all states participated.

Representatives and direct Taxes shall be apportioned among the several States which may be included within this Union, according to their respective Numbers, which shall be determined by adding to the whole Number of free Persons, including those bound to Service for a Term of Years, and excluding Indians not taxed, three fifths of all other Persons.

The actual Enumeration shall be made within three Years after the first Meeting of the Congress of the United States, and within every subsequent Term of ten Years, in such Manner as they shall by Law direct. The Number of Representatives shall not exceed one for every thirty Thousand, but each State shall have at Least one Representative; and until such enumeration shall be made, the State of New Hampshire shall be entitled to choose three, Massachusetts eight, Rhode Island and Providence Plantations one, Connecticut five, New York six, New Jersey four, Pennsylvania eight, Delaware one, Maryland six, Virginia ten, North Carolina five, South Carolina five and Georgia three.

apportion. v. to split up and assign

Southern states wanted slaves ("other Persons") to count as three-fifths of a person so they could have more representatives in Congress but not pay more in taxes.

enumeration. n. official count of the population; census

In the House of Representatives, representation is based on population. States with more people get to elect more representatives.

When vacancies happen in the Representation from any State, the Executive Authority thereof shall issue Writs of Election to fill such Vacancies.

The House of Representatives shall choose their Speaker and other Officers; and shall have the sole Power of Impeachment.

impeachment. n. accusation of misconduct against an official

SECTION 3

The Senate of the United States shall be composed of two Senators from each State, chosen by the Legislature thereof, for six Years; and each Senator shall have one Vote.

Every state gets two senators, no matter its population.

Immediately after they shall be assembled in Consequence of the first Election, they shall be divided as equally as may be into three Classes. The Seats of the Senators of the first Class shall be vacated at the Expiration of the second Year, of the second Class at the Expiration of the fourth Year, and of the third Class at the Expiration of the sixth Year, so that one third may be chosen every second Year;

and if Vacancies happen by Resignation, or otherwise, during the Recess of the Legislature of any State, the Executive thereof may make temporary Appointments until the next Meeting of the Legislature, which shall then fill such Vacancies.

No person shall be a Senator who shall not have attained to the Age of thirty Years, and been nine Years a Citizen of the United States, and who shall not, when elected, be an Inhabitant of that State for which he shall be chosen.

The Vice President of the United States shall be President of the Senate, but shall have no Vote, unless they be equally divided.

The Senate shall choose their other Officers, and also a President pro tempore, in the absence of the Vice President, or when he shall exercise the Office of President of the United States.

appointment. n.
the assignment of a job or position to a person, rather than by election

Every two years, one-third of the Senate is up for reelection.

Wait, this is a confusing double negative. It simply means you have to be at least 30 and live in the state you represent.

The Senate shall have the sole Power to try all Impeachments. When sitting for that Purpose, they shall be on Oath or Affirmation. When the President of the United States is tried, the Chief Justice shall preside: And no Person shall be convicted without the Concurrence of two thirds of the Members present.

concurrence. n. same opinion; agreement

Judgment in Cases of Impeachment shall not extend further than to removal from Office, and disqualification to hold and enjoy any Office of honor, Trust or Profit under the United States: but the Party convicted shall nevertheless be liable and subject to Indictment, Trial, Judgment and Punishment, according to Law.

SECTION 4

The Times, Places and Manner of holding Elections for Senators and Representatives, shall be prescribed in each State by the Legislature thereof; but the Congress may at any time by Law make or alter such Regulations, except as to the Place of Choosing Senators.

The Congress shall assemble at least once in every Year, and such Meeting shall be on the first Monday in December, unless they shall by Law appoint a different Day.

> Congress actually meets way more than once a year!

SECTION 5

Each House shall be the Judge of the Elections, Returns and Qualifications of its own Members, and a Majority of each shall constitute a Quorum to do Business; but a smaller number may adjourn from day to day, and may be authorized to compel the Attendance of absent Members, in such Manner, and under such Penalties as each House may provide.

adjourn. n. to break from a meeting

Each House may determine the Rules of its Proceedings, punish its Members for disorderly Behavior, and, with the Concurrence of two-thirds, expel a Member.

Each House shall keep a Journal of its Proceedings, and from time to time publish the same, excepting such Parts as may in their Judgment require Secrecy; and the Yeas and Nays of the Members of either House on any question shall, at the Desire of one fifth of those Present, be entered on the Journal.

Neither House, during the Session of Congress, shall, without the Consent of the other, adjourn for more than three days, nor to any other Place than that in which the two Houses shall be sitting.

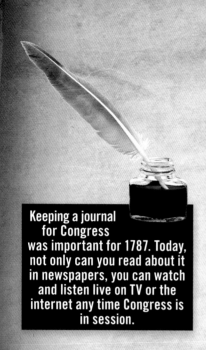

Keeping a journal for Congress was important for 1787. Today, not only can you read about it in newspapers, you can watch and listen live on TV or the internet any time Congress is in session.

SECTION 6

compensation. n. money awarded for service; payment

The Senators and Representatives shall receive a Compensation for their Services, to be ascertained by Law, and paid out of the Treasury of the United States. They shall in all Cases, except Treason, Felony and Breach of the Peace, be privileged from Arrest during their Attendance at the Session of their respective Houses, and in going to and returning from the same; and for any Speech or Debate in either House, they shall not be questioned in any other Place.

No Senator or Representative shall, during the Time for which he was elected, be appointed to any civil Office under the Authority of the United States which shall have been created, or the Emoluments whereof shall have been increased during such time; and no Person holding any Office under the United States, shall be a Member of either House during his Continuance in Office.

They can't make up a new job for themselves.

emoluments. n. salary

SECTION 7

All bills for raising Revenue shall originate in the House of Representatives; but the Senate may propose or concur with Amendments as on other Bills.

revenue. n. income; in this case, tax money

These are all the steps for a bill to become a law.

Every Bill which shall have passed the House of Representatives and the Senate, shall, before it become a Law, be presented to the President of the United States; If he approve he shall sign it, but if not he shall return it, with his Objections to that House in which it shall have originated, who shall enter the Objections at large on their Journal, and proceed to reconsider it. If after such Reconsideration two thirds of that House shall agree to pass the Bill, it shall be sent, together with the Objections, to the other House, by which it shall likewise be reconsidered, and if approved by two thirds of that House, it shall become a Law. But in all such Cases the Votes of both Houses shall be determined by Yeas and Nays, and the Names of the Persons voting for and against the Bill shall be entered on the Journal of each House respectively. If any Bill shall not be returned by the President within ten Days (Sundays excepted) after it shall have been presented to him, the Same shall be a Law, in like Manner as if he had signed it, unless the Congress by their Adjournment prevent its Return, in which Case it shall not be a Law.

Every Order, Resolution, or Vote to which the Concurrence of the Senate and House of Representatives may be necessary (except on a question of Adjournment) shall be presented to the President of the United States; and before the Same shall take Effect, shall be approved by him, or being disapproved by him, shall be repassed by two thirds of the Senate and House of Representatives, according to the Rules and Limitations prescribed in the Case of a Bill.

Here's what Congress can do! In addition to making laws for the country, they can also deal with money, make post offices, and protect copyright and patents.

SECTION 8

The Congress shall have Power To lay and collect Taxes, Duties, Imposts and Excises, to pay the Debts and provide for the common Defence and general Welfare of the United States; but all Duties, Imposts and Excises shall be uniform throughout the United States;

To borrow money on the credit of the United States;

duty. n. a tax on imported goods

Collecting taxes allowed the Federal Government to do more for its people.

counterfeit. v.
to imitate with fraud

tribunal. n. court

To regulate Commerce with foreign Nations, and among the several States, and with the Indian Tribes;

To establish an uniform Rule of Naturalization, and uniform Laws on the subject of Bankruptcies throughout the United States;

To coin Money, regulate the Value thereof, and of foreign Coin, and fix the Standard of Weights and Measures;

To provide for the Punishment of counterfeiting the Securities and current Coin of the United States;

To establish Post Offices and Post Roads;

To promote the Progress of Science and useful Arts, by securing for limited Times to Authors and Inventors the exclusive Right to their respective Writings and Discoveries;

To constitute Tribunals inferior to the supreme Court;

To define and punish Piracies and Felonies committed on the high Seas, and

Offenses against the Law of Nations; To declare War, grant Letters of Marque and Reprisal, and make Rules concerning Captures on Land and Water;

Letter of Marque and Reprisal. n. a license to attack enemy ships and bring their crews to court.

To raise and support Armies, but no Appropriation of Money to that Use shall be for a longer Term than two Years;

To provide and maintain a Navy;

To make Rules for the Government and Regulation of the land and naval Forces;

To provide for calling forth the Militia to execute the Laws of the Union, suppress Insurrections and repel Invasions;

To provide for organizing, arming, and disciplining, the Militia, and for governing such Part of them as may be employed in the Service of the United States, reserving to the States respectively, the Appointment of the Officers, and the Authority of training the Militia according to the discipline prescribed by Congress;

They planned for a national capital, what would someday become Washington, D.C. When George Washington was president, the White House wasn't built yet. The capital city bounced around a bit, since Congress met in different places.

To exercise exclusive Legislation in all Cases whatsoever, over such District (not exceeding ten Miles square) as may, by Cession of particular States, and the acceptance of Congress, become the Seat of the Government of the United States, and to exercise like Authority over all Places purchased by the Consent of the Legislature of the State in which the Same shall be, for the Erection of Forts, Magazines, Arsenals, dock-Yards, and other needful Buildings; And

To make all Laws which shall be necessary and proper for carrying into Execution the foregoing Powers, and all other Powers vested by this Constitution in the Government of the United States, or in any Department or Officer thereof.

SECTION 9

The Migration or Importation of such Persons as any of the States now existing shall think proper to admit, shall not be prohibited by the Congress prior to the Year one thousand eight hundred and eight, but a tax or duty may be imposed on such Importation, not exceeding ten dollars for each Person.

The privilege of the Writ of Habeas Corpus shall not be suspended, unless when in Cases of Rebellion or Invasion the public Safety may require it.

Many northerners wanted to end slavery, but southerners didn't. This got both sides very fired up. The writers compromised with this section. It says importing slaves can't be made illegal for 20 years.

writ of habeas corpus. n. the requirement that a person be told why he or she is being held under arrest.

If you're arrested you must be told why. This is a protection against unlawful imprisonment.

Only a court can find someone guilty of a crime, and a punishment can't be changed after a crime is committed.

No Bill of Attainder or ex post facto Law shall be passed.

No capitation, or other direct, Tax shall be laid, unless in Proportion to the Census or Enumeration herein before directed to be taken.

No Tax or Duty shall be laid on Articles exported from any State.

commerce. n. the activity of buying and selling goods

No Preference shall be given by any Regulation of Commerce or Revenue to the Ports of one State over those of another: nor shall Vessels bound to, or from, one State, be obliged to enter, clear, or pay Duties in another.

The people have a right to know where their tax money is going!

No Money shall be drawn from the Treasury, but in Consequence of Appropriations made by Law; and a regular Statement and Account of the Receipts and Expenditures of all public Money shall be published from time to time.

appropriation. n. money assigned for a particular use

No Title of Nobility shall be granted by the United States: And no Person holding any Office of Profit or Trust under them, shall, without the Consent of the Congress, accept of any present, Emolument, Office, or Title, of any kind whatever, from any King, Prince or foreign State.

nobility. n. a group of people identified as being of a superior class

We aren't a monarchy! We aren't going to act like that!

SECTION 10

No State shall enter into any Treaty, Alliance, or Confederation; grant Letters of Marque and Reprisal; coin Money; emit Bills of Credit; make any Thing but gold and silver Coin a Tender in Payment of Debts; pass any Bill of Attainder, ex post facto Law, or Law impairing the Obligation of Contracts, or grant any Title of Nobility.

The U.S. is all one country. States can't just work with other countries on their own or create their own money.

We just finished fighting with England over taxes! Let's make sure taxes are fair.

No State shall, without the Consent of the Congress, lay any Imposts or Duties on Imports or Exports, except what may be absolutely necessary for executing its inspection Laws: and the net Produce of all Duties and Imposts, laid by any State on Imports or Exports, shall be for the Use of the Treasury of the United States; and all such Laws shall be subject to the Revision and Control of the Congress.

No State shall, without the Consent of Congress, lay any duty of Tonnage, keep Troops, or Ships of War in time of Peace, enter into any Agreement or Compact with another State, or with a foreign Power, or engage in War, unless actually invaded, or in such imminent Danger as will not admit of delay.

ARTICLE 2.

SECTION 1

The executive Power shall be vested in a President of the United States of America. He shall hold his Office during the Term of four Years, and, together with the Vice-President chosen for the same Term, be elected, as follows:

Each State shall appoint, in such Manner as the Legislature thereof may direct, a Number of Electors, equal to the whole Number of Senators and Representatives to which the State may be entitled in the Congress: but no Senator or Representative, or Person holding an Office of Trust or Profit under the United States, shall be appointed an Elector.

Article 2 outlines the presidency: How one is elected, what the job is all about, and how the president can get kicked out!

FUN FACT

It wasn't until 13 years after declaring independence that the United States elected a president, in 1789.

WASHINGTON

The Electors shall meet in their respective States, and vote by Ballot for two persons, of whom one at least shall not lie an Inhabitant of the same State with themselves. And they shall make a List of all the Persons voted for, and of the Number of Votes for each; which List they shall sign and certify, and transmit sealed to the Seat of the Government of the United States, directed to the President of the Senate. The President of the Senate shall, in the Presence of the Senate and House of Representatives, open all the Certificates, and the Votes shall then be counted. The Person having the greatest Number of Votes shall be the President, if such Number be a Majority of the whole Number of Electors appointed; and if there be more than one who have such Majority, and have an equal Number of Votes, then the House of Representatives shall immediately choose by Ballot one of them for President; and if no Person have a Majority, then from the five highest on the List the said House shall in like Manner choose the President. But in choosing the President, the Votes shall be taken by States, the Representation from each State having one Vote; a quorum for this Purpose shall consist of a Member or Members from two-thirds of the States, and a Majority of all the States shall be necessary to a Choice. In every Case, after the Choice of the President, the Person having the greatest Number of Votes of the Electors shall be the Vice President. But if there should remain two or more who have equal Votes, the Senate shall choose from them by Ballot the Vice-President.

The Congress may determine the Time of choosing the Electors, and the Day on which they shall give their Votes; which Day shall be the same throughout the United States.

quorum. n. the minimum number of voting members to make a meeting official

The original plan was for the runner-up to be Vice President. That might not always make for a "perfect union." This was later changed by the twelfth amendment.

The president must be a U.S. citizen from birth who is 35 or older and has lived in the United States for 14 years. And there's more to it than that, of course!

devolve. v. transfer power to a lower level

No person except a natural born Citizen, or a Citizen of the United States, at the time of the Adoption of this Constitution, shall be eligible to the Office of President; neither shall any Person be eligible to that Office who shall not have attained to the Age of thirty-five Years, and been fourteen Years a Resident within the United States.

In Case of the Removal of the President from Office, or of his Death, Resignation, or Inability to discharge the Powers and Duties of the said Office, the same shall devolve on the Vice President, and the Congress may by Law provide for the Case of Removal, Death, Resignation or Inability, both of the President and Vice President, declaring what Officer shall then act as President, and such Officer shall act accordingly, until the Disability be removed, or a President shall be elected.

The President shall, at stated Times, receive for his Services, a Compensation, which shall neither be increased nor diminished during the Period for which he shall have been elected, and he shall not receive within that Period any other Emolument from the United States, or any of them.

Before he enter on the Execution of his Office, he shall take the following Oath or Affirmation:

"I do solemnly swear (or affirm) that I will faithfully execute the Office of President of the United States, and will to the best of my Ability, preserve, protect and defend the Constitution of the United States."

affirmation. n. a sworn promise about future behavior

FUN FACT

New Hampshire was the ninth state to ratify the Constitution, making it the law of the land in 1788.

SECTION 2

Section 2 lists the jobs of the president.

The President shall be Commander in Chief of the Army and Navy of the United States, and of the Militia of the several States, when called into the actual Service of the United States; he may require the Opinion, in writing, of the principal Officer in each of the executive Departments, upon any subject relating to the Duties of their respective Offices, and he shall have Power to Grant Reprieves and Pardons for Offenses against the United States, except in Cases of Impeachment.

He shall have Power, by and with the Advice and Consent of the Senate, to make Treaties, provided two thirds of the Senators present concur; and he shall nominate, and by and with the Advice and Consent of the Senate, shall appoint Ambassadors, other public Ministers and Consuls, Judges of the supreme Court, and all other Officers of the United States, whose Appointments are not herein otherwise provided for, and which shall be established by Law: but the Congress

reprieve. n. the cancellation or postponement of a punishment

treaty. n. a formal agreement between countries

ambassador. n. a person acting as a country's official representative in a foreign country

may by Law vest the Appointment of such inferior Officers, as they think proper, in the President alone, in the Courts of Law, or in the Heads of Departments.

The President shall have Power to fill up all Vacancies that may happen during the Recess of the Senate, by granting Commissions which shall expire at the End of their next Session.

Many people think presidents can do whatever they want, but they often have to ask permission from Congress first.

SECTION 3

He shall from time to time give to the Congress Information of the State of the Union, and recommend to their Consideration such Measures as he shall judge necessary and expedient; he may, on extraordinary Occasions, convene both Houses, or either of them, and in Case of Disagreement between them, with Respect to the Time of Adjournment, he may adjourn them to such Time as he shall think proper; he shall receive Ambassadors and other public Ministers; he shall take Care that the Laws be faithfully executed, and shall Commission all the Officers of the United States.

SECTION 4

The President, Vice President and all civil Officers of the United States, shall be removed from Office on Impeachment for, and Conviction of, Treason, Bribery, or other high Crimes and Misdemeanors.

Congress can "fire" a president, vice-president, or judge if they feel they did something very wrong.

ARTICLE 3.

SECTION 1

The judicial Power of the United States, shall be vested in one supreme Court, and in such inferior Courts as the Congress may from time to time ordain and establish. The Judges, both of the supreme and inferior Courts, shall hold their Offices during good Behavior, and shall, at stated Times, receive for their Services a Compensation which shall not be diminished during their Continuance in Office.

Article 3 explains the court system and the most important Supreme Court. That court can decide if laws are justified and fair under the Constitution. Any decision made there will affect the whole country.

FUN FACT

The Constitution never says how many judges the court should have (today there are nine) or what qualifications they must have.

SECTION 2

The judicial Power shall extend to all Cases, in Law and Equity, arising under this Constitution, the Laws of the United States, and Treaties made, or which shall be made, under their Authority; to all Cases affecting Ambassadors, other public Ministers and Consuls; to all Cases of admiralty and maritime Jurisdiction; to Controversies to which the United States shall be a Party; to Controversies between two or more States; between a State and Citizens of another State; between Citizens of different States; between Citizens of the same State claiming Lands under Grants of different States, and between a State, or the Citizens thereof, and foreign States, Citizens or Subjects.

FUN FACT

The Supreme Court was around for 145 years before it got a permanent home, a court house in Washington, D.C.

Some-one who is unhappy with a court decision can "appeal" to a higher court. It's like asking for a do-over from a more powerful judge. The Supreme Court of the United States is the last stop!

In all Cases affecting Ambassadors, other public Ministers and Consuls, and those in which a State shall be Party, the supreme Court shall have original Jurisdiction. In all the other Cases before mentioned, the supreme Court shall have appellate Jurisdiction, both as to Law and Fact, with such Exceptions, and under such Regulations as the Congress shall make.

The Trial of all Crimes, except in Cases of Impeachment, shall be by Jury;

FUN FACT

William Howard Taft is the only person who served as a U.S. president and a Supreme Court justice.

and such Trial shall be held in the State where the said Crimes shall have been committed; but when not committed within any State, the Trial shall be at such Place or Places as the Congress may by Law have directed.

SECTION 3

Treason against the United States, shall consist only in levying War against them, or in adhering to their Enemies, giving them Aid and Comfort. No Person shall be convicted of Treason unless on the Testimony of two Witnesses to the same overt Act, or on Confession in open Court.

The Congress shall have power to declare the Punishment of Treason, but no Attainder of Treason shall work Corruption of Blood, or Forfeiture except during the Life of the Person attainted.

Article 4
is all about how
states interact
with each other
and how they work
with the Federal
Government.

ARTICLE 4.

SECTION 1

Full Faith and Credit shall be given in each State to the public Acts, Records, and judicial Proceedings of every other State. And the Congress may by general Laws prescribe the Manner in which such Acts, Records and Proceedings shall be proved, and the Effect thereof.

"Full faith and credit" means that states should recognize each other's laws.

felony. n. a crime regarded as very serious

SECTION 2

The Citizens of each State shall be entitled to all Privileges and Immunities of Citizens in the several States.

A Person charged in any State with Treason, Felony, or other Crime, who shall flee from Justice, and be found in another State, shall on demand of the executive Authority of the State from which he fled, be delivered up, to be removed to the State having Jurisdiction of the Crime.

No Person held to Service or Labour in one State, under the Laws thereof, escaping into another, shall, in Consequence of any Law or Regulation therein, be discharged from such Service or Labour, But shall be delivered up on Claim of the Party to whom such Service or Labour may be due.

This part is about slavery again, saying if enslaved people escape to a different state, that state must return them.

A Map of the
UNITED STATES
OF
AMERICA,
with Part of the
ADJOINING PROVINCES
from the latest Authorities.

SECTION 3

New States may be admitted by the Congress into this Union; but no new States shall be formed or erected within the Jurisdiction of any other State; nor any State be formed by the Junction of two or more States, or parts of States, without the Consent of the Legislatures of the States concerned as well as of the Congress.

The Congress shall have Power to dispose of and make all needful Rules and Regulations respecting the Territory or other Property belonging to the United States; and nothing in this Constitution shall be so construed as to Prejudice any Claims of the United States, or of any particular State.

SECTION 4

The United States shall guarantee to every State in this Union a Republican Form of Government, and shall protect each of them against Invasion; and on Application of the Legislature, or of the Executive (when the Legislature cannot be convened) against domestic Violence.

You mean, I can't just declare my back-yard to be the new state of "Coolifornia"?

republican. adj. relating to a government whose people elect representatives

We're all in this together, so we gotta look out for each other! If any state gets attacked, the whole United States will fight back.

domestic. adj. relating to one's own country. In this case, "domestic violence" means fighting from within the states, rather than war with another country.

ARTICLE 5.

The Congress, whenever two thirds of both Houses shall deem it necessary, shall propose Amendments to this Constitution, or, on the Application of the Legislatures of two thirds of the several States, shall call a Convention for proposing Amendments, which, in either Case, shall be valid to all Intents and Purposes, as part of this Constitution, when ratified by the Legislatures of three fourths of the several States, or by Conventions in three fourths thereof, as the one or the other Mode of Ratification may be proposed by the Congress; Provided that no Amendment which may be made prior to the Year One thousand eight hundred and eight shall in any Manner affect the first and fourth Clauses in the Ninth Section of the first Article; and that no State, without its Consent, shall be deprived of its equal Suffrage in the Senate.

Article 5 is all about how to amend, or make changes to, the Constitution. This isn't easy, but really important!

amendment. n. an official change

ratification. n. the act of officially accepting or agreeing

suffrage. n. the right to vote

There are the rules about slaves, again! You can't change the rules about importing enslaved people until 1808. Oh, and you can't change that every state gets the same number of senators.

ARTICLE 6.

The United States owed money, and Article 6 pretty much said "Don't worry, we're still going to pay you back."

All Debts contracted and Engagements entered into, before the Adoption of this Constitution, shall be as valid against the United States under this Constitution, as under the Confederation.

This Constitution, and the Laws of the United States which shall be made in Pursuance thereof; and all Treaties made, or which shall be made, under the Authority of the United States, shall be the supreme Law of the Land; and the Judges in every State shall be bound thereby, any Thing in the Constitution or Laws of any State to the Contrary notwithstanding.

The president, congressmen, and judges didn't have to believe in God to do their job, but they did have to agree to support the Constitution.

The Senators and Representatives before mentioned, and the Members of the several State Legislatures, and all executive and judicial Officers, both of the United States and of the several States, shall be bound by Oath or Affirmation, to support this Constitution; but no religious Test shall ever be required as a Qualification to any Office or public Trust under the United States.

ARTICLE 7.

The Ratification of the Conventions of nine States, shall be sufficient for the Establishment of this Constitution between the States so ratifying the Same.

Done in Convention by the Unanimous Consent of the States present the Seventeenth Day of September in the Year of our Lord one thousand seven hundred and Eighty seven and of the Independence of the United States of America the Twelfth. In Witness whereof We have hereunto subscribed our Names.

> As soon as nine states agree to this Constitution, that's when it starts!

George Washington
PRESIDENT AND DEPUTY
FROM VIRGINIA

NEW HAMPSHIRE

John Langdon,
Nicholas Gilman

MASSACHUSETTS

Nathaniel Gorham
Rufus King

CONNECTICUT

William Samuel
Johnson,
Roger Sherman

NEW YORK

Alexander Hamilton

NEW JERSEY

William Livingston,
David Brearley.
William Paterson,
Jonathan Dayton

PENNSYLVANIA

Benjamin Franklin,
Thomas Mifflin,
Robert Morris.
George Clymer
Thomas Fitzsimons,
Jared Ingersoll
James Wilson,
Gouverneur Morris

DELAWARE

George Read,
Gunning Bedford Jr.
John Dickinson,
Richard Bassett.
Jacob Broom

MARYLAND

James McHenry.
Daniel of St Thomas Jenifer
Daniel Carroll

VIRGINIA

John Blair
James Madison Jr.

NORTH CAROLINA

William Blount.
Richard Dobbs Spaight.
Hugh Williamson

SOUTH CAROLINA

John Rutledge.
Charles Cotesworth Pinckney.
Charles Pinckney.
Pierce Butler

GEORGIA

William Few,
Abraham Baldwin

ATTEST:

William Jackson
SECRETARY

INTRODUCTION TO THE BILL OF RIGHTS

After the convention of 1787 crafted and approved the Constitution, three-fourths of the states needed to have their own legislatures vote to approve the document. This didn't all come easily though, as many thought the new Constitution was illegal since the existing congress didn't write it. Other people were concerned the new central government took too much power away from the states.

The biggest problem that people saw, however, was that the new Constitution didn't spell out what rights belonged to the people. Many of the delegates had to go back to their states to defend the document and try to convince their legislatures to adopt it. Federalists, who supported the new Constitution, insisted it was clear that any powers that the Constitution didn't give to the government were powers of the people. But that wasn't good enough for the anti-Federalist critics. In many states, people demanded a bill of rights that would clearly show the limits of government power, something Americans had seen abused under the English crown.

Not wanting to throw away all the work they had done, Federalists began to promise the first task of a Congress under the new Constitution would be to craft such a list. Only then did many states agree to adopt the Constitution.

Instead of changing the actual wording of the Constitution, any changes, called amendments, would appear separately after article seven. Many amendments were proposed by Congress at that time but, after much discussion and debate, ten were approved by enough states to become official. The Bill of Rights is what we call those first ten amendments.

4

THE Conventi

declaratory and restrictive clauses shoul

RESOLVED

be proposed to the Legislatures of the several Co

ts and purposes, as part of the said Co

ARTICLES in addition

rticle of the original Constitution.

d by the first Article of the Cons

alated by Congress

shall am

THE U.S. BILL OF RIGHTS

THE PREAMBLE TO THE BILL OF RIGHTS

Congress of the United States begun and held at the City of New-York, on Wednesday the fourth of March, one thousand seven hundred and eighty nine.

THE Conventions of a number of the States, having at the time of their adopting the Constitution, expressed a desire, in order to prevent misconstruction or abuse of its powers, that further declaratory and restrictive clauses should be added: And as extending the ground of public confidence in the Government, will best ensure the beneficent ends of its institution.

RESOLVED by the Senate and House of Representatives of the United States of America, in Congress assembled, two thirds of both Houses concurring, that the following Articles be proposed to the Legislatures of the several States, as amendments to the Constitution of the United States, all, or any of which Articles, when ratified by three fourths of the said Legislatures, to be valid to all intents and purposes, as part of the said Constitution; viz.

ARTICLES in addition to, and Amendment of the Constitution of the United States of America, proposed by Congress, and ratified by the Legislatures of the several States, pursuant to the fifth Article of the original Constitution.

AMENDMENT 1

Congress shall make no law respecting an establishment of religion, or prohibiting the free exercise thereof; or abridging the freedom of speech, or of the press; or the right of the people peaceably to assemble, and to petition the Government for a redress of grievances.

grievance. n. a wrongdoing or unfair treatment

People can peacefully get together and protest, speaking freely without worry about their words getting them arrested. There can't be an official religion, and different religions are protected.

FUN FACT

James Madison was the principal author of the Constitution. He also wrote the first set of amendments.

AMENDMENT 2

A well regulated Militia, being necessary to the security of a free State, the right of the people to keep and bear Arms, shall not be infringed.

AMENDMENT 3

No Soldier shall, in time of peace be quartered in any house, without the consent of the Owner, nor in time of war, but in a manner to be prescribed by law.

militia. n. an army made up of civilians

People were skeptical of powerful governments and armies, so they wanted to be armed if anyone threatened to take control. The "right to bear arms" means citizens may keep weapons.

British soldiers could go into people's houses and camp out even when war wasn't happening. Amendment 3 was Congress' way of saying "we're better than that and won't invade your space."

AMENDMENT 4

Amend-
ment 4 tells
us that police
must have and
show a reason to
search your house
for something.
It's a way of
protecting
individuals
from unfair
policing.

The right of the people to be secure in their persons, houses, papers, and effects, against unreasonable searches and seizures, shall not be violated, and no Warrants shall issue, but upon probable cause, supported by Oath or affirmation, and particularly describing the place to be searched, and the persons or things to be seized.

AMENDMENT 5

Have
you heard
about
someone
"pleading the
fifth" in court?
It means you can
choose to say
nothing instead
of something
that might get
yourself in
trouble.

No person shall be held to answer for a capital, or otherwise infamous crime, unless on a presentment or indict-ment of a Grand Jury, except in cases arising in the land or naval forces, or in the Militia, when in actual service in time of War or public danger; nor shall any person be subject for the same offense to be twice put in jeopardy of life or limb; nor shall be compelled in any criminal case to be a witness against himself, nor be deprived of life, liberty, or property, without due process of law; nor shall private property be taken for public use, without just compensation.

AMENDMENT 6

In all criminal prosecutions, the accused shall enjoy the right to a speedy and public trial, by an impartial jury of the State and district wherein the crime shall have been committed, which district shall have been previously ascertained by law, and to be informed of the nature and cause of the accusation; to be confronted with the witnesses against him; to have compulsory process for obtaining witnesses in his favor, and to have the Assistance of Counsel for his defence.

This all stands to make sure justice is fair and true. The government or judges can't misbehave if the trial is public! Also, a trial must happen near the place of the crime.

AMENDMENT 7

In Suits at common law, where the value in controversy shall exceed twenty dollars, the right of trial by jury shall be preserved, and no fact tried by a jury, shall be otherwise re-examined in any Court of the United States, than according to the rules of the common law.

Most people would see the judgement of a jury to be more fair than a decision made by one judge. This is why this right is so important!

It's a right to all people, even those accused and found guilty of crimes, to be treated fairly!

AMENDMENT 8

Excessive bail shall not be required, nor excessive fines imposed, nor cruel and unusual punishments inflicted.

AMENDMENT 9

The enumeration in the Constitution, of certain rights, shall not be construed to deny or disparage others retained by the people.

It would be impossible to list every right a person has. Just because they aren't all in here, doesn't mean they don't exist! For instance, these include your right to travel and right to vote.

FUN FACT

Two proposed amendments weren't adopted by the states. One of them finally passed in 1992, more than two hundred years later! This amendment stated that members of Congress couldn't vote themselves a raise until after the next election. The other proposed amendment, which would say how large the House of Representatives should be, never passed.

AMENDMENT 10

The powers not delegated to the United States by the Constitution, nor prohibited by it to the States, are reserved to the States respectively, or to the people.

Okay, so the Constitution spells out a lot of stuff the U.S. government can do. Anything else the Constitution doesn't mention can be up to the states to decide.

FUN FACT
One of George Washington's jobs as president was to send the list of twelve proposed amendments to each state to have their leaders vote on them.

THE PATRIOTS
BIOS OF REVOLUTIONARY REBELS

JOHN ADAMS

1735-1826

BORN IN BRAINTREE, MASSACHUSETTS

EDUCATION: HARVARD COLLEGE

OCCUPATION: PROMINENT BOSTON LAWYER

KNOWN FOR: Helping to craft the Declaration of Independence and serving as the first U.S. vice president and second U.S. president.

OTHER ACHIEVEMENTS: It wasn't popular, but he defended in court the British soldiers on trial for firing into a crowd of Bostonians in what came to be known as the Boston Massacre. He also wrote about splitting up government power into three branches, created the Massachusetts constitution, and was one of America's first ambassadors in Europe.

PERSONAL DETAILS: Married to Abigail (Smith) Adams and father of four children. Both John Adams and Thomas Jefferson died July 4, 1826, on the fiftieth anniversary of the Declaration of Independence. John Adams' eldest child, John Quincy Adams, became the sixth U.S. president.

MEMORABLE QUOTE: "Facts are stubborn things; and whatever may be our wishes, our inclinations, or the dictates of our passions, they cannot alter the state of facts and evidence." —defense arguments in the Boston Massacre trial, 1770

ABIGAIL SMITH ADAMS

1744-1818

BORN IN: WEYMOUTH, MASSACHUSETTS

EDUCATION: NO FORMAL EDUCATION, BUT A VORACIOUS READER WHO WAS CURIOUS AND LEARNED MUCH ON HER OWN.

OCCUPATION: FARMER AND MOTHER

KNOWN FOR: Writing outspoken letters back and forth to her husband, John Adams. He often sought her advice on matters.

OTHER ACHIEVEMENTS: She supported her family and their farm while her husband was working on creating the Declaration of Independence or in Europe serving as an American ambassador.

PERSONAL DETAILS: She and John had four children, including John Quincy, who would go on to become the sixth president. When John Adams was serving as American minister to France, Abigail joined him and wrote about her dislike of the rigid rules of European society.

MEMORABLE QUOTE: "I long to hear that you have declared an independency—and by the way in the New Code of Laws… I desire you would Remember the Ladies, and be more generous and favourable to them than your ancestors." —in a letter to husband John Adams, March 1776

PAUL REVERE

1735-1818

BORN IN BOSTON, MASSACHUSETTS

EDUCATION: SCHOOLED UNTIL HE WAS 13, WHEN HE BECAME AN APPRENTICE TO HIS FATHER, A SILVERSMITH.

OCCUPATION: SILVERSMITH, MILITIA OFFICER

KNOWN FOR: Establishing an early alert system to warn colonial militias of British army activity. A famous poem recounts Revere's horse ride through the night announcing the army's advance toward Lexington and Concord.

OTHER ACHIEVEMENTS: Member of rebellious "Sons of Liberty" who kept watch over ships in Boston Harbor and participated in the Boston Tea Party. Produced numerous engravings and propaganda to support rebel causes.

MEMORABLE QUOTE: "The regulars are coming out!" —an alert to those along the route to Lexington of the approaching British army

SYBIL LUDINGTON

1761-1839

BORN IN KENT, NEW YORK

KNOWN FOR: As a teenager, riding through the night to warn minutemen of the April 26, 1777 British attack on Danbury, Connecticut.

PERSONAL DETAILS: Often compared to Paul Revere, Sybil was the oldest daughter of Colonel Henry Ludington, the commander of the local militia. To try to save Danbury from burning to the ground, sixteen-year-old Sybil rode her horse Star through the night for forty miles, knocking on doors to muster, or gather, the militia for the fight. By morning, nearly four hundred men were ready to fight. Sybil was praised for her bravery, and General George Washington even visited to thank her in person. Today a statue of Sybil stands as a memorial, and historical markers follow her route through Putnam County, New York.

MEMORABLE QUOTE: "The British are burning Danbury! Muster at Ludington's!"

CRISPUS ATTUCKS

1723-1770

BORN IN FRAMINGHAM, MASSACHUSETTS

OCCUPATION: SAILOR, DOCK WORKER

KNOWN FOR: The first man killed in the Boston Massacre, and therefore the Revolutionary War. Attucks was among a rowdy mob that John Adams later called a "motley rabble of saucy boys." The crowd taunted and threw ice and rocks at British soldiers, who then fired in defense, killing five including Attucks.

PERSONAL DETAILS: Little is known for certain, but historians believe Attucks' father was an African slave and his mother a Wampanoag native American. Attucks likely escaped slavery himself in his twenties, and spent much of his adult life as a sailor on whaling ships. He probably felt threatened by the British presence in Boston, since off-duty soldiers might compete for part-time work at low wages.

PATRICK HENRY

1736-1799

BORN IN HANOVER COUNTY, VIRGINIA

EDUCATION: ATTENDED GRAMMAR SCHOOL BEFORE BEING TUTORED BY HIS FATHER.

OCCUPATION: PLANTER, LAWYER, GOVERNOR OF VIRGINIA

KNOWN FOR: Convincing other Virginia legislators to support revolution and to fight against the king's army.

OTHER ACHIEVEMENTS: Speaking out against King George, even a decade before the revolutionary war. His speech in the Virginia colony assembly was called "treasonous" by his colleagues. Introduced the Virginia Resolves, an early protest against taxes from England. At first an anti-Federalist opposed to the Constitution, he pushed hard for a bill of rights and thereafter supported the Constitution.

PERSONAL DETAILS: Once believed to have only married into land-wealth, Henry's family was well off. He tried his hand in business and planting but had few successes.

MEMORABLE QUOTE: "Is life so dear, or peace so sweet, as to be purchased at the price of chains and slavery? Forbid it, Almighty God! I know not what course others may take; but as for me, give me liberty, or give me death!" —speech before House of Burgesses on March 23, 1775

SAMUEL ADAMS

1722-1803

BORN IN BOSTON, MASSACHUSETTS

EDUCATION: HARVARD

OCCUPATION: ACCOUNTANT, BREWER, TAX COLLECTOR, POLITICAL PHILOSOPHER, POLITICIAN

KNOWN FOR: Organizing the Sons of Liberty, a group of rebels who caused trouble in Boston for the British by destroying their goods and starting fights. This inspired other groups to pop up and actively rebel against the British. He wrote many letters and spoke out against British tyranny. He signed his letters using many different names, which gave the ideas a more popular appearance (the names included Vindex the Avenger, Candidus, Populus, and Determinatus).

OTHER ACHIEVEMENTS: Governor of Massachusetts, 1793–1797

PERSONAL DETAILS: Samuel Adams didn't have a thriving career but held many different occupations during his life. He was most successful at complaining about the British. He had six children and struggled to support his family financially.

MEMORABLE QUOTE: "The spark of liberty then kindles into a flame; when the injured people attentive to the feelings of their just rights magnanimously contend for their compleat restoration." —October 4, 1790

GEORGE WASHINGTON

1732-1799

BORN IN WESTMORELAND COUNTY, VIRGINIA

EDUCATION: MINIMAL FORMAL EDUCATION. WITH A GIFT FOR MATHEMATICS, HE LEARNED SURVEYING AS AN APPRENTICE.

OCCUPATION: SURVEYOR, ARMY GENERAL, AND THE FIRST U.S. PRESIDENT

KNOWN FOR: Leading the Continental Army to victory in the American Revolution and becoming the first president of the United States.

OTHER ACHIEVEMENTS: Presided over the Constitutional Convention in 1787. Widely respected as a leader, Washington is the the only president to be elected unanimously by the electoral college—twice!

PERSONAL DETAILS: Married Martha Custis, who brought with her great inherited land holdings.

MEMORABLE QUOTE: "Discipline is the soul of an army. It makes small numbers formidable; procures success to the weak, and esteem to all." —letter of instructions to Virginia company captains, 1759

MARTHA CUSTIS WASHINGTON

1731–1802

BORN IN NEW KENT COUNTY, VIRGINIA

OCCUPATION: FIRST LADY (ALTHOUGH THE TITLE DIDN'T YET EXIST!)

KNOWN FOR: Wife of General (and later, President) George Washington

OTHER ACHIEVEMENTS: Kept morale up among U.S. Army officers while camped at Valley Forge for the winter. She also served as hostess, receiving other guests to the winter home at the military camp for eight years.

MEMORABLE QUOTE: "I think I am more like a state prisoner than anything else" —expressing displeasure with her role as first lady

MERCY OTIS WARREN

1728-1814

BORN IN BARNSTABLE, MASSACHUSETTS

EDUCATION: NO FORMAL SCHOOLING, BUT STUDIED WITH HER BROTHERS AS THEY PREPARED FOR HARVARD COLLEGE.

OCCUPATION: WRITER, PLAYWRIGHT

KNOWN FOR: Writing poems and plays that attacked royal authority and supported independence.

OTHER ACHIEVEMENTS: Often writing under a pseudonym (false name), she argued against ratifying the U.S. Constitution because it lacked a bill of rights. After 1790, she wrote a book of poems and plays using her own real name, which was extremely rare for a woman at that time.

PERSONAL DETAILS: Mercy's husband James was a busy and important political figure in Massachusetts. She was good friends with Martha Washington and Abigail and John Adams and would often exchange letters with each discussing matters related to the revolution and their new country.

MEMORABLE QUOTE: "America stands armed with resolution and virtue; but she still recoils at the idea of drawing the sword against the nation from whence she derived her origin. Yet Britain, like an unnatural parent, is ready to plunge her dagger into the bosom of her affectionate offspring." —letter to Catharine Macaulay, December 29, 1774

ROGER SHERMAN

1721-1793

BORN IN NEWTON, MASSACHUSETTS

EDUCATION: GRAMMAR SCHOOL, BUT HIS FATHER KEPT AN EXTENSIVE LIBRARY AND HE READ OFTEN.

KNOWN FOR: Signer of the Declaration of Independence, Articles of Confederation, and the U.S. Constitution. One of the "Committee of Five" to draft the Declaration.

OTHER ACHIEVEMENTS: Despite having no law schooling, Sherman passed the bar exam in Connecticut and served as a judge at several important levels. He was also a U.S. representative and senator for Connecticut.

MEMORABLE QUOTE: "Their being candidates for re-election will probably be one of the most powerful motives, (next to that of their virtue) to fidelity in office, and by that means alone would they hope for success." —predicting why Senators will behave themselves, in a letter to John Adams, 1789

ELIZABETH "MUM BETT" FREEMAN

ABOUT 1742-1829

BORN IN CLAVERACK, NEW YORK

OCCUPATION: FORMER ENSLAVED SERVANT

KNOWN FOR: Fighting for and winning her freedom in Massachusetts court under the state's new constitution.

OTHER ACHIEVEMENTS: Her lawsuit would lead to the abolition of slavery in Massachusetts.

PERSONAL DETAILS: Born to enslaved parents, Mum Bett was sold when she was only six months old. She served the same master for nearly forty years. After poor treatment, she ran away and sought protection by the law. She had heard the new Massachusetts constitution and Bill of Rights stated that "All men are born free and equal," and thought—rightly—that it must be true for her as well!

MEMORABLE QUOTE: "Any time while I was a slave, if one minute's freedom had been offered to me, and I had been told I must die at the end of that minute, I would have taken it—just to stand one minute on God's earth a free woman—I would." —as told to Catharine Sedgewick, a writer and the daughter of Freeman's lawyer

THOMAS JEFFERSON

1743-1826

BORN IN SHADWELL, VIRGINIA

EDUCATION: A BUSY READER WHO LEARNED FRENCH, GREEK, AND LATIN FROM AGE NINE. HE STUDIED AT VIRGINIA'S COLLEGE OF WILLIAM & MARY.

OCCUPATION: LAWYER, PLANTATION OWNER

KNOWN FOR: Writing the Declaration of Independence, serving as third president of the United States

OTHER ACHIEVEMENTS: Acted as one of the new United States' first ministers (ambassador) to France. As president, he approved the Louisiana Purchase, which doubled the size of the country. Later, he founded the University of Virginia.

PERSONAL DETAILS: Thomas and his wife Martha inherited a large amount of land, as well as slaves who worked on it. He died on July 4, 1826—the fiftieth anniversary of the Declaration of independence, and the same day as his friend John Adams.

MEMORABLE QUOTE: "I see my job as trying to bring together and harmonize a variety of different opinions. We are putting before all of mankind words that are both simple and firm, a justification for the stand that we're being forced to take." —on writing the Declaration of Independence

THOMAS PAINE

1737-1809

BORN IN: THETFORD, ENGLAND

EDUCATION: GRAMMAR SCHOOL IN ENGLAND, FOLLOWED BY APPRENTICESHIP TO HIS FATHER.

OCCUPATION: ROPEMAKER

KNOWN FOR: Authoring "Common Sense," a 1776 pamphlet that charged up American colonists and built the case for independence.

OTHER ACHIEVEMENTS: Along with Benjamin Franklin, Paine negotiated financial support for the American Revolutionary War from France.

PERSONAL DETAILS: Bouncing from job to job in England, Paine met Benjamin Franklin, who suggested he move to the American colonies.

MEMORABLE QUOTE: "In England a king hath little more to do than to make war and give away places; which in plain terms, is to impoverish the nation and set it together by the ears." —from "Common Sense," 1776

EMILY GEIGER

ABOUT 1763-1793

BORN IN SOUTH CAROLINA

KNOWN FOR: As a young woman, Emily Geiger volunteered to carry secret instructions from American army General Nathaniel Greene to General Thomas Sumter, one hundred miles away through British-controlled land. She was captured, but while the British loyalists summoned a woman to search her, Emily had enough time to read and memorize the message. She then tore up the note—and ate it! When no papers were found, Emily was released and able to travel on to tell the message and her exciting tale!

PERSONAL DETAILS: An only child whose father was too sick or frail to fight in the army, Emily Geiger sought out a chance to help the revolution effort as a messenger.

BENJAMIN FRANKLIN

1706-1790

BORN IN BOSTON, MASSACHUSETTS

EDUCATION: FORMAL SCHOOL AT BOSTON LATIN SCHOOL IN HIS EARLY YEARS, APPRENTICED AS A PRINTER, AND SELF-TAUGHT AFTER THAT.

OCCUPATION: PRINTER, DIPLOMAT

KNOWN FOR: So much! Way more than a kite flyer and the face on the $100 bill, Franklin is best known for his roles as a scientist, inventor, printer, and all-around patriot. He helped to draft the Declaration of Independence, and he also signed the Constitution.

OTHER ACHIEVEMENTS: Benjamin Franklin is credited with building the alliance with France during the revolution. He is known for inventing bifocals and the lightning rod.

PERSONAL DETAILS: Like many in his day, Ben Franklin wrote under a pseudonym, or pen name. This meant new ideas could be published and spread without any risk of harm to the author from those who might disagree. Some of his early letters were signed "Silence Dogood," a middle-aged widow of his own creation.

MEMORABLE QUOTE: "…if all Printers were determin'd not to print any thing till they were sure it would offend no body, there would be very little printed." —from the 1731 essay "An Apology for Printers"

ESTHER DE BERDT REED

1746-1780

BORN IN LONDON, ENGLAND

EDUCATION: INSTRUCTED BY HER FATHER IN A STRICT RELIGIOUS TRADITION.

OCCUPATION: MOTHER, WRITER, ACTIVIST

KNOWN FOR: Publishing an essay titled "Sentiments of an American Woman" to call women to action to support the men in the army.

OTHER ACHIEVEMENTS: Founded "Ladies of Philadelphia" and raised huge amounts of money to support struggling soldiers, which George Washington suggested be spent on new clothes. The women hand-made all the shirts.

PERSONAL DETAILS: Esther met her American husband Joseph Reed while he studied law in London. After marrying in 1770 in London, they moved to Philadelphia. Split between loyalties to her homeland and her new home, Esther grew upset by the way England treated the colonies. As the war escalated, Joseph became an army general, and Esther cared for their six children while also working on her patriotic efforts.

MEMORABLE QUOTE: "I think the cause in which he is engaged so just, so glorious, and I hope so victorious." —on her husband's fighting in the Revolutionary War

JOHN HANCOCK

1737-1793

BORN IN BRAINTREE, MASSACHUSETTS

EDUCATION: HARVARD

OCCUPATION: MERCHANT, POLITICIAN

KNOWN FOR: His big signature on the Declaration of Independence—as the president of the Continental Congress, it was fitting that he be the first to sign this document.

OTHER ACHIEVEMENTS: Having amassed great wealth from family and as a businessman, Hancock is recognized for funding much of the revolutionary acts in Boston.

PERSONAL DETAILS: John Hancock's mother was left destitute by the death of her husband. John went to live with his wealthy aunt and uncle, Lydia and Thomas Hancock on Beacon Hill in Boston. When his uncle died, John Hancock inherited his wealth. He enjoyed his wealth but also was a philanthropist, donating much money to help the needy and improve the city of Boston.

MEMORABLE QUOTE: "I have the most animating confidence that the present noble struggle for liberty will terminate gloriously for America." —address on the anniversary of the Boston Massacre

MARGARET COCHRAN CORBIN

1751-1800

BORN IN WESTERN PENNSYLVANIA

KNOWN FOR: Fighting in battle alongside her husband, and continuing to fight after his death and her own injury.

OTHER ACHIEVEMENTS: Margaret Cochran Corbin is recognized as the first woman to "take a soldier's part in the war for liberty." She was also the first woman to receive a military pension, although she was given only one-half of the amount a man would receive.

PERSONAL DETAILS: Orphaned from age five, Margaret was raised by her uncle. In 1772 she married John Corbin, who would join the militia some years later. Following her husband to war, Margaret usually cleaned, cooked, and cared for soldiers. During the Battle at Fort Washington in November 1776, Margaret went to the battlefield with her husband. John was killed in battle while loading his cannon, so Margaret stepped in to take his place. She was wounded multiple times. The British forces won the battle, but Margaret Corbin's cannon was firing until the very end.

JAMES MADISON

1751–1836

BORN IN: PORT CONWAY, VIRGINIA

EDUCATION: UNDER PRIVATE TUTORAGE, STUDIED HISTORY, GOVERNMENT, LAW, AND LATIN. ATTENDED WHAT IS NOW PRINCETON UNIVERSITY.

OCCUPATION: LEGISLATOR AND FOURTH PRESIDENT OF THE UNITED STATES

KNOWN FOR: Writing much of the U.S. Constitution and Bill of Rights.

OTHER ACHIEVEMENTS: Served as Secretary of State for Thomas Jefferson, and together they completed the Louisiana Purchase from France.

PERSONAL DETAILS: Madison was the smallest U.S. president, at only five feet, four inches tall, and never weighing over 100 pounds. He married Dolley Payne, a widow, when he was forty-three years old, which was quite late in life at that time.

MEMORABLE QUOTE: "The accumulation of all powers, legislative, executive, and judiciary, in the same hands, whether of one, a few, or many, and whether hereditary, self-appointed, or elective, may justly be pronounced the very definition of tyranny." —*The Federalist* Papers, No. 47, February 1, 1788

BETSY ROSS

1752-1836

BORN IN WEST JERSEY, PENNSYLVANIA

EDUCATION: PUBLIC QUAKER SCHOOL, THEN APPRENTICED TO AN UPHOLSTERER.

OCCUPATION: UPHOLSTERER (SEAMSTRESS)

KNOWN FOR: Family legend claims Betsy Ross created the first American flag for General George Washington, including the design of a five-pointed star.

OTHER ACHIEVEMENTS: While her husband John served in the Pennsylvania militia, Betsy made tents and blankets and repaired military uniforms. Betsy and John likely knew General Washington well through church and militia connections.

PERSONAL DETAILS: Raised in a large Quaker family, Betsy fell in love and at age twenty-one eloped with another apprentice, John Ross. This led to her expulsion from the Quaker church and society, but the two established an upholstery business together. John Ross was killed in the war, and Betsy remarried twice.

BENEDICT ARNOLD

1741–1801

BORN IN: NORWICH, CONNECTICUT

EDUCATION: PRIVATE GRAMMAR SCHOOL. DESTINED FOR YALE, HIS CHANCES DISAPPEARED WITH THE LOSS OF FAMILY FORTUNE.

OCCUPATION: BUSINESSMAN, MERCHANT, CONTINENTAL ARMY GENERAL

KNOWN FOR: Defecting to the British Army and plotting to surrender West Point.

OTHER ACHIEVEMENTS: Despite successes in his military career, Arnold felt he had been unfairly passed over by the Continental Congress for promotions. In the United States, his name has become synonymous with betrayal.

MEMORABLE QUOTE: "I am now led to devote my life to the re-union of the British empire, as the best and only means to dry up the streams of misery that have deluged this country." —letter "To the Inhabitants of America," 1780

"355"

AGENT 355 was a female spy who was part of the Culpher Ring, an intelligence group that helped to expose Benedict Arnold's treachery. 355 was the code number for "lady."

OTHER ACHIEVEMENTS: Agent 355's true identity was never discovered and many historians have tried to reveal who she really was. She was a mysterious figure in the Revolution.

PERSONAL DETAILS: She is believed to come from a Loyalist family and would had access to important information about British actions in and around New York during the Revolutionary War.

TEACHING WITH THIS BOOK

This book can be used in many different ways. Our hope is that learners of all ages will gain a better understanding of the importance of these revolutionary documents, how they influenced the formation of the United States, and how they still impact us today.

ESSENTIAL QUESTIONS
- Why do we have rules?
- Why do people break rules? When is it okay to break rules?
- What makes rules fair?
- How does the U.S. Constitution affect my life today?

PRE-READING ACTIVITIES

Examine some primary sources from the colonial and revolutionary era, without reading deeply into their content. Focus on text features and allow students to make observations about the typeset, handwriting, artwork, or organization and how they might differ from modern letters or printed material.

Show a larger map of the original 13 colonies. Compare and contrast that map to a map of the East Coast of the United

States today. Point out the distance across the Atlantic Ocean to England. How long would it have taken people to travel in the late 1700s?

WHILE READING

SMALL GROUP DISCUSSION

Which arguments for independence seem the strongest, as written in the Declaration?

CLOSE READING

Identify unfamiliar terms in the Preamble to the Constitution and make predictions about their meanings.

DISCUSS

What does the preamble actually say and mean?
What is its purpose?

VOCABULARY STUDY

Organize key vocabulary terms using simple definitions, synonyms, and pictorial representation.

FIRST PERSON

Read and discuss primary source accounts from both patriots and loyalists to understand the conflicting feelings and multiple perspectives in the country during this time.

MATH CONNECTION

Create a timeline that accurately places important events in revolutionary history in order, spaced to scale.

WRITING CONNECTION

The first amendment guarantees freedom of religion, freedom of speech, freedom of the press, the right to peacefully assemble, and the right to protest the government. Which of these rights is most important to you?

EXTENSION ACTIVITIES

Create a classroom constitution to establish expectations and security in your own classroom. Drawing from a list of answers to the essential question "Why do we have rules?" generate a preamble to your own classroom constitution. Have students sign the bottom to demonstrate their support, and hang the document prominently in the classroom for all to see.

Analyze other amendments to the Constitution that were adopted later. Why did these changes happen when they did?

CREATIVE WRITING

Write a declaration of independence from the perspective of a family pet. What grievances would be aired about its treatment under your reign?

HELPFUL WEBSITES TO FIND MORE PRIMARY SOURCES AND INFORMATION

- Library of Congress: http://www.loc.gov
- The National Archives: http://www.archives.gov
- National Humanities Center: http://americainclass.org/primary-sources

ABOUT THE AUTHORS

JJ Prior grew up in Weymouth, Massachusetts, also the birthplace and hometown of Abigail Adams. He holds a master's degree in education and is a fifth grade teacher in Keene, New Hampshire. JJ enjoys photography and the outdoors and spends much of his time lost in thought.

Emilia Whippie Prior teaches the fifth and sixth grades in a small-town school in New Hampshire. She was born and raised near Keene, New Hampshire, also the hometown of Barry Faulkner, who painted the murals above the Declaration and Constitution in the National Archives building. Emilia has degrees in education and social sciences, with a focus in history and geography. She enjoys traveling, arts, theatre, and inspiring her students.

The husband-and-wife team live in a 1781 colonial farmhouse. This is their first book.

ABOUT APPLESAUCE PRESS BOOK PUBLISHERS

Good ideas ripen with time. From seed to harvest, Applesauce Press brings fine reading, information, and entertainment together between the covers of its creatively crafted books. Our Cider Mill bears fruit twice a year, publishing a new crop of titles each spring and fall.

VISIT US ON THE WEB AT
www.cidermillpress.com

OR WRITE TO US AT
PO Box 454
12 Spring Street
Kennebunkport, Maine 04046